WRITING EXTRAVAGANZA!

Journal Prompts & Story Starters for Creative Teens

Senior Edition

Asheville Bellingham Ithaca

Writing Extravaganza!
Journal Prompts and Story Starters for Creative Teens, Senior Ed.
Second Edition

Copyright © 2020, 2022 by The Playhard Project

Published by The Playhard Press
The Playhard Press is an imprint of The Playhard Project LLC.

Matthew Barrington, Managing Director
Margaret Ellis, Series Editor
Abdul MuQeet, Graphic Design
Steven B. Dodson, Operations Consultant
Chelsea Cooper, Strategy Consultant

All Rights Reserved. No part of this publication may be reproduced, stored in a retrieval system, or transmitted in any form or by any means, electronic, mechanical, photocopying, recording, or otherwise, without written permission of the publisher.

This book is a work of fiction. Names, characters, places, and incidents are either the product of the author's imagination or are used fictitiously, and any resemblance to actual persons, living or dead, business establishments, events, or locales is entirely coincidental.

playhardpress.com
playhardproject.com
writingextravaganza.com

ISBN 978-1-954305-15-1

Dedication

To Mrs. Bohrer

Kevin & Eugene

and The Crooked Path

Whether the weather is cold
Or whether the weather is hot
Whatever the weather, we're in this together
Whether we like it or not!

Welcome!

To the greatest writing book ever!

What is a Writing Extravaganza anyway?

It's like a circus with a bunch of different acts all under the same big tent. Variety is the spice of life—and this book is super spicy! There are oodles of different prompts to easily get your creative sparks flying.

What's inside?

There are story starters that are taken from the actual lives of real teens. There are prompts that explore the best of times and the worst of times, the opposites found in life, and a little bit of everything in between. Some prompts daydream about if you could do something, while others get real because you know you can't. There are poetry challenges, true crime stories, ideas to get to the bottom of problems, and different ways to think about stuff, too. There are letters to yourself in the future and the past, pages to drain your brain, tons of deep thoughts, and much, much more!

How does it work?

There is no wrong way to use this book! Flip through and find something that speaks to you, then go for it! Don't hold back—this book is for you to get it all out! You can write *anything* you want, *anywhere* you want, *anytime* you want, about *anybody* you want, *anyway* you want! There are no rules: Just write! And write! And write! And write! And write! And write!

I'm going to be living in the dorms next year. All the rooms are shared. That means I'm going to have a roommate who I don't know. I'm worried about the worst-case scenario happening. But what about the best-case scenario? Here's how life could play out…

If I Could Freeze...

If I could freeze the hands of time for just one day, I would capitalize on every minute by doing all the things I've always wanted, like first...

_____
_____
_____
_____
_____
_____
_____
_____
_____
_____
_____
_____
_____
_____
_____
_____
_____
_____
_____
_____

But I Can't!

But I can't freeze time. Time is always slowly slipping by. It's an easy thing to waste. Here are some earnest examples of both wise and poor uses of my time...

Good Uses of Time	*Bad Uses of Time*
_____	_____
_____	_____
_____	_____
_____	_____
_____	_____
_____	_____
_____	_____
_____	_____

If you managed your time better, what awesome new things could you make time for in your life?

_____
_____
_____
_____
_____

A Letter to

Write a letter to your future self. What advice do you want to tell future you? Any predictions? What are all the things you hope you don't forget? Remind yourself about what is most important to you in life.

the Future

There was this party out in the country and somehow we ended up there at the end of the night. There were a bunch of people drinking from red plastic cups and climbing this big, old tree in front of the house. They looked super high up and were swaying back and forth, singing and laughing. Then we heard this loud sound...

My Family's Best

The best things about being a part of my family and our family dynamics are...

_____
_____
_____
_____
_____
_____
_____
_____

Describe all the ways that you contribute to the good things that you like about your family...

_____
_____
_____
_____
_____
_____
_____

My Family's Worst

The worst things about being a member of my family and our family interactions might be...

___
___
___
___
___
___
___

Explore different ways you could do your part to improve the things you don't like about your family...

___
___
___
___
___
___
___

Of all the things you wrote, which one is the easiest to do? Could it make a difference? Would it hurt to try?

___
___

Fitting In

These are all the things I do to fit in…

_____
_____
_____
_____
_____
_____
_____

Illustrate a time in your life when you felt like you really fit in…

_____
_____
_____
_____
_____
_____
_____
_____

Standing Out

Here are all the things I do to stand out...

_____
_____
_____
_____
_____
_____
_____

Write about a time in your life when you really stood out from the crowd...

_____
_____
_____
_____
_____
_____
_____
_____
_____

We always met up at the park before heading to school in the morning. Kevin and Joni were sitting at the picnic table as usual. But something was wrong. Kevin looked super serious and said to me, "We're not going to school today. Today, we're on a mission from God." I'm sorry, what? They explained...

If I Could Change...

If I could change how I acted in a recent situation, I totally would! Here are the details of what happened:

_____
_____
_____
_____
_____

What led up to this situation? Did anything trigger you?

_____
_____
_____

What were the thoughts in your head at the time?

_____
_____
_____

What emotions or feelings were you experiencing?

_____ _____ _____
_____ _____ _____
_____ _____

Feeling & Emotion Vocabulary Wheel in the back of the book!

But I Can't!

But I can't change how I acted. Here's how I feel now about the choices I made:

_____
_____
_____
_____

How did other people react? How did they feel?

_____
_____

I can think of a number of strategies that I can use to handle similar situations in the future. Here's my plan:

_____
_____
_____
_____
_____

My Imagination

Let's use the power of our imagination to create a relaxing, peaceful scene. You know how your heart speeds up when you're watching an action movie? Your brain knows it's not real, but your body still has a reaction! In the same way, we can trick our brains into doing just the opposite—by imagining a relaxing place, our bodies can feel like we're actually there! The secret is to use all five of your senses.

First, choose the most relaxing place in the world that you can possibly imagine:

_____

Next, list out absolutely everything about your place that you can sense—really dive in and describe all the little details!

I can see: _____

I can hear: _____

I can feel: _____

I can smell: _____

I can taste: _____

Mini Vacation

Last, put yourself in the scene. Where are you and what are you doing? Use all those sensory details to paint the most vivid picture you can! The more detailed you make it, the more you can trick your mind into thinking you're actually there—and the more relaxed and better you'll feel!

_____
_____
_____
_____
_____
_____
_____
_____
_____
_____
_____
_____
_____

Now that you created this vivid, calming scene—close your eyes and imagine you are there! Return to this special place to take a mini vacation whenever you need a break from your busy life. The more you practice this, the easier it becomes!

I used to be a bad person. When my parents raised me, they put their prejudice in my heart. But then one day when I was a senior, I went to this huge party. I looked across the room and there they were. I couldn't stop staring at them and they couldn't take their eyes off of me. I had finally met my destiny...

_____
_____
_____
_____
_____
_____
_____
_____
_____
_____
_____
_____
_____
_____
_____

Writing My

The one, the only—the story of your life! As told by the author themselves, this dramatic retelling is taking the world by storm. Give your unique perspective on the major events of your life. How has your life unfolded? Do you dare to write about your life in the future? Start with a fitting title and tell your story to the world!

Autobiography

Lies I've Told

These are some of the most regrettable ways I have been deceitful to other people...

_____
_____
_____

Sometimes people carry around feelings of guilt or shame that haunt them like a ghost. If you feel bad about something—it's never too late to repair the damage. You could always apologize and do something nice for the people that were hurt like:

_____
_____
_____
_____
_____
_____

Can you promise yourself that you won't repeat the same mistakes in the future? If you can start to accept what happened, the ghost of regret will be free to go.

Lies Told to Me

Here are some of the most hurtful ways that other people have been deceitful to me...

___
___
___
___
___

When we're lied to, we get angry. But anger doesn't ride alone! Underlying feelings are hidden beneath our anger. For example, if we feel hurt? We're angry! Feel jealous? Angry! Feel let down? Again—angry! Think about these lies or times you've been angry recently—can you find which other emotions were behind it?

___
___
___
___
___

Feeling & Emotion Vocabulary Wheel in the back of the book!

I'm so close to the end of school, I can taste it! When I graduate, I'm going to make sure that the poor underclassmen have it easier than me. I need a way to pass on all the things I have learned. I'll bequeath...

If I Could Make...

If I could make just one of my hard problems disappear, the most impactful one that I would choose to get rid of is...

_____

_____

_____

_____

Here's how I imagine that my life would be different if it were suddenly just gone:

_____

_____

_____

_____

_____

_____

_____

_____

_____

_____

But I Can't!

But I can't just wish that a real problem will go away on its own. I can explore the pros and cons of doing something versus doing nothing about it, like this:

	Pros	Cons
Doing Something	Pros of trying different things to fix a problem	Cons of trying different things to fix a problem
Doing Nothing	Pros of doing nothing to fix a problem	Cons of doing nothing to fix a problem

Based on your answers, would it be better to live with the problem or give it your best shot?

_____

_____

Poet's Choice

Write a poem about a favorite moment from your life:

Poet's Challenge
The Shakespearian Sonnet

The kind of sonnet that Shakespeare liked to write now bears his name. First, he wrote three sections with four lines each (called quatrains) that had an alternate rhyme. Then, he finished the sonnet by tying a nice little bow at the end, using a couplet. His rhyme scheme looks like this: ABAB CDCD EFEF GG. If you really want an extra challenge, Shakespeare also made sure that each line had ten syllables that followed a regular rhythm—daDUM daDUM daDUM daDUM daDUM—but the rhyming is hard enough! Start with a topic you feel passionate about. The couplet at the end usually sums up the poem's main idea. Some poets think a strong couplet at the end is a good place to start. Begin however you like!

_____ A
_____ B
_____ A
_____ B
_____ C
_____ D
_____ C
_____ D
_____ E
_____ F
_____ E
_____ F
_____ G
_____ G

All the different cliques of people in our grade are kind of coming together this year and bonding in a way that they never have before. Maybe it's because we're all going our separate ways soon. I can't believe who I saw laughing, arm in arm today...

_____
_____
_____
_____
_____
_____
_____
_____
_____
_____
_____
_____
_____
_____
_____
_____
_____

If I Could Mindread...

If I could read other people's minds without their knowledge, I would finally have the upper hand! I would use my new psychic power to...

_____
_____
_____
_____
_____
_____
_____
_____
_____
_____
_____

With great power comes great responsibility—how did you choose to use yours? For good or for yourself?

_____
_____
_____

But I Can't!

But I can't read minds. I don't actually know what anyone is thinking or if they're even thinking about me at all. How often does your mind jump to conclusions?

_____
_____
_____

How would you rate yourself on being assertive in your communication—you know, being confident and self-assured, but without being too aggressive?

_____
_____
_____

When you want to know what someone is thinking or feeling—or when you think you know and you don't like it—you can keep it inside, or you can speak up. List some things you want to be more assertive about:

_____
_____
_____
_____
_____

Eugene was telling this story about how he was on his bike and he got hit by a car. He said that he died that day and now he's just a walking dead body. Nobody believed him because that's crazy, but I secretly saw something that happened today that made me second guess myself. Eugene was...

Love & Kindness

The best thing that another living soul has ever had the heart to do for me was...

___

Have you been inspired to do any random acts of kindness for anyone recently? What's seriously the best thing you think you've ever done for someone?

___

Pain & Suffering

The worst thing that another human being has ever had the hatred and malice to do to me was...

_____
_____
_____
_____
_____
_____
_____
_____

When people hold on to pain, it turns into suffering. We can't change what happened in the past. Would accepting things as they are help people to let go of some of the hurt that they carry around inside?

_____
_____
_____
_____

A Wasted Life

Write about your perspective on what it means for a person to squander or waste their life...

_____
_____
_____
_____
_____
_____
_____
_____
_____
_____
_____
_____

What are some negative beliefs that would lead a person astray, to live an empty or meaningless life?

_____   _____   _____
_____   _____   _____
_____   _____   _____

A Life Well-Lived

Explain your viewpoint on what it means for a person to self-actualize or live their life to the fullest...

_____
_____
_____
_____
_____
_____
_____
_____
_____
_____

What are some core values or beliefs that would guide a person to live a rich, fulfilling life?

_____	_____	_____
_____	_____	_____
_____	_____	_____
_____	_____	_____
_____	_____	

Core Values List in the back of the book!

Senior Prom was right around the corner. I was all set to go, but now I suddenly found myself without a date. Do I even want to go now? Things felt hopeless. But then, something unexpected happened. I was cramming for a test in the library when...

If I Could Go Back...

If I could go back to my freshman year and live high school all over again, here's what I would do...

_____
_____
_____
_____
_____
_____
_____
_____
_____
_____
_____
_____
_____
_____
_____
_____

I guess this means some hidden regrets I have are:

_____   _____
_____   _____

But I Can't!

But I can't go back and relive my life—I can only press forward! If I can come to terms with my past, I can grow from it. From this point onward, here's how I'm going to choose to live my days...

_____
_____
_____
_____
_____
_____
_____
_____
_____

Here are some regrets that I want to make sure I don't end up having in the future:

_____
_____
_____

Write a wonderful adventure about this majestic reindeer philosopher from the far reaches of the snowy Arctic Circle…

My parents aren't sold on what I want to major in. I need to convince them that this is what I want to do with my life. I decided to come up with a list of reasons why this major is good for me—and a list of arguments against all the reasons that they think I should do something else. The next time we sit down to talk about it, I can respectfully explain...

Pro Tip— Writing out all the things you want to say will really help you in a conversation. When we're put on the spot, we tend to forget all the great things we wanted to say! It's totally okay to have notes with you during an important talk.

The Best of Me

The best things about being who I am as an individual in our society are...

_____
_____
_____
_____
_____
_____
_____

How did you come to believe all of these great things? Describe the times when people complimented you or told you these positive things about yourself:

_____
_____
_____
_____
_____
_____
_____

The Worst of Me

The worst things about being who I am as a person might be...

_____
_____
_____
_____

How we think that other people view us—changes our view of ourselves. But is what we think that they think even really true? Or do we make it up in our heads sometimes? How often do you engage in mindreading?

_____
_____
_____
_____

Is it fair to use other people's judgements to measure our self-worth? I mean, who are they to say, anyway? Whose opinions do you value the most? Should you?

_____
_____
_____
_____

Past Changes

These are the greatest changes that I have already weathered in my life...

_____
_____
_____
_____
_____
_____
_____
_____

Sometimes we don't realize all the changes we've gone through! How have some of these changes made you a stronger, more resilient person?

_____
_____
_____
_____
_____
_____
_____

Changes Ahead

Here are some impending changes that I'll have to undoubtably deal with in the future...

_____
_____
_____
_____
_____
_____
_____

Ever stop to think that you've made it through 100% of all your bad days? How can all the things that you've overcome bolster confidence for the changes ahead?

_____
_____
_____
_____
_____
_____

Our parents finally let us drive to the big city alone to see our friends in college. After eating in a restaurant, we were driving back to the dorms. Erin's car was following behind us—the car that I almost decided to ride in—and they turned too soon into traffic. An oncoming car hit them head-on and glass went flying! We slammed on the breaks and...

If I Could Love...

If I could be in a relationship with anyone in school or college, here's how I imagine our blissful, romantic life together would be...

_____
_____
_____
_____
_____
_____
_____
_____
_____
_____
_____
_____
_____
_____
_____
_____
_____
_____
_____
_____

But I Can't!

But I can't cast a spell and be in a relationship with anyone I want. Instead, here's what I can do to let people know that I'd like to get to know them better...

_____
_____
_____
_____

Would you want someone to be direct and honest with you about how they felt? Would you respect them more for it? If you could be real with someone about how you felt, would it give you more self-respect?

_____
_____
_____
_____

Rejection happens to everyone. It can be awkward, no doubt. How can you deal with rejection gracefully?

_____
_____
_____

Problem?

Describe a problem you are facing in detail:

_____
_____
_____
_____
_____
_____
_____

First, write down *three possible choices* to deal with the problem. Then, list all the advantages and the disadvantages of each choice.

Choice #1: _____

_____

Advantages of #1	Disadvantages of #1
_____	_____
_____	_____
_____	_____
_____	_____

Solution!

Choice #2: _____

_____

Advantages of #2	Disadvantages of #2
_____	_____
_____	_____
_____	_____
_____	_____

Choice #3: _____

_____

Advantages of #3	Disadvantages of #3
_____	_____
_____	_____
_____	_____
_____	_____

What does your heart tell you to do? _____

What does your brain tell you to do? _____

The best solution to the problem is: _____

Tim always asked, but Lillian always said "no." It went on and on like this, day after day. Then one day, it went too far. Lillian was ready to take matters into her own hands once and for all. She...

Full Head?

The thoughts in your brain flow like a river or stream. This is a game to empty those thoughts from your head and let them flow onto the paper. Here's how to play—write every thought you have on these pages. Anything that comes to mind! No stopping. No thinking about what you're writing. Forget about spelling and mess ups—just keep going. Your hand starts to hurt? Keep going! You think it sounds stupid? Write that down and keep going! Whatever you do, don't stop writing the real-time thoughts, feelings, and comments your brain is making. Think you can make it to the bottom of the next page?

Ready? Get set—Flow!

_____

_____

_____

_____

_____

_____

_____

_____

_____

_____

_____

Brain Drain!

_____
_____
_____
_____
_____
_____
_____
_____
_____
_____
_____
_____
_____
_____
_____
_____
_____
_____
_____
_____

Stop! Now ask yourself—how do I feel? This is a great way to release all the stuff that you didn't even know was weighing you down. Try it anytime your head feels too full or too busy!

Admiration

Cast some light on the things, qualities, or people for which you have the most admiration...

_____
_____
_____
_____
_____
_____
_____
_____
_____

What are some small things that you can do to take on more of the qualities that you admire?

_____
_____
_____
_____

Disgust

Talk about the ideas, traits, or people that you loathe and are most disgusted by...

_____
_____
_____
_____

How can unpleasant feelings kickstart people into some sort of positive action? How could you turn your disgust into a launch-pad for motivation or change?

_____
_____
_____
_____
_____
_____
_____
_____

Jacob was partying every weekend now. He had a restaurant job where he could swipe whatever he wanted. At first it was fun, but now it's all he ever wants to do. He started to ignore his friends. Soon, they began ignoring him, too. But his oldest friends decided they aren't giving up so easy. One evening...

Brain on Autopilot?

When something bad happens, the first thought that pops into our mind is usually negative. Thanks a lot, brain! 🙄 What are some negative things your brain might say to you in the following situations:

You make a poor grade on a test.
Negative Thought ➡ _____

A friend invites someone else over, not you.
Negative Thought ➡ _____

The teacher embarrasses you in front of the class.
Negative Thought ➡ _____

You get made fun of because of _____ .
_{Fill in the Blank}
Negative Thought ➡ _____

You get caught doing something wrong.
Negative Thought ➡ _____

The person you like doesn't like you.
Negative Thought ➡ _____

Do you know the worst part about thinking these things? They're not even true! It's just our brain on autopilot, saying negative stuff. But when we hear these things in our head, guess what? It makes us feel bad about ourselves. And who wants that?

Nope, I'm the Pilot!

You are the pilot that gets to steer your brain—not the other way around. Changing those autopilot thoughts can change how you feel overall. Let's take the same situations and write a better thought to replace it:

Okay, so I made a bad grade on a test…

A Better Thought ➡ _____

So my friend invited someone else over this time…

A Better Thought ➡ _____

I got embarrassed in front of everyone, but…

A Better Thought ➡ _____

Just because they made fun of me…

A Better Thought ➡ _____

Okay, I got caught doing something I shouldn't…

A Better Thought ➡ _____

The person I like doesn't like me the same way…

A Better Thought ➡ _____

Now you know that negative thoughts are what pop up first—and you know that they're not really true! The game is to catch them, stop them, and change them to something that serves you better. This little action boosts our self-esteem in a huge way. Try it!

The Letter

Write a letter that will never be sent. Say all the things you want to say to someone—but can't! Be honest. Get all of your feelings off your chest. Release your bottled up emotions and put them down on the page.

to No One

Warning! Do not give this letter to anyone, no matter how much you think you want to. This is for you, not for them! Don't do it!

Jade's parents were out of the country for the entire summer. We ended up hanging out at her place a lot. We even started going there when she was still at work. One night, Jade came home tired from work to find a bunch of us partying inside. She dropped her bag and suddenly broke down in tears. She...

The Best

The best things about my body and outward physical appearance are...

___
___
___
___
___
___
___

Is beauty determined by your body—or is it better portrayed by your heart, your mind, and your spirit?

___
___
___
___
___
___
___
___

The Worst

The worst things about my body and outward physical characteristics might be...

_____
_____
_____
_____

Your worth is not tied to your physical appearance. 💯 By whose standards of good looks or beauty are you holding yourself up to? Is it fair to compare yourself to celebrities or influencers on social media?

_____
_____
_____
_____

How much time do you spend worrying about society's ideal standards of beauty instead of doing things that actually make you happy? Is it worth all your effort?

_____
_____
_____
_____

Isolated

These are some times in my life when I have felt at my loneliest and most isolated…

_____

_____

_____

The next time I start to feel this way, I can plan to…

Talk to these people: _____

_____

_____

Listen to my favorite music: _____

_____

_____

Distract myself with these activities: _____

_____

Distraction List in the back of the book!

_____

Tell myself these positive things: _____

_____

_____

My own ideas: _____

Connected

Here are other times in my life when I have felt the most loved, supported, or connected with others...

_____
_____
_____
_____
_____

The time is always right to tell people that you're glad they're in your life. Here are ways I can show others how much I appreciate their friendship and love:

_____
_____
_____
_____
_____
_____
_____
_____

One of my friends is considering joining the Army after they graduate—but they're not so sure. It's a big decision, for real. They say that the Army recruiter keeps calling and asking them to sign the enlistment papers. We needed to talk to a veteran who actually knew about all this stuff firsthand, so we got in the car and drove out on a mission…

If I Could Fly Away...

If I could grow enormous wings and soar far, far away from this place, I would...

_____
_____
_____
_____
_____
_____
_____
_____
_____
_____
_____
_____
_____
_____

I guess these are the things I wish I could escape:

_____   _____
_____   _____

But I Can't!

But I can't just fly away. I can blow off some steam and vent about why I feel like escaping sometimes...

_____
_____
_____
_____
_____
_____
_____
_____
_____
_____

Refusing to accept things in your life doesn't change your situation. It can actually add to painful feelings. Are there any realities you can try to stop fighting?

_____
_____
_____
_____
_____

My Five Year

One year from now I'd like...

To be: _____
To have: _____
To let go: _____
To give: _____

Two years from now I'd like...

To be: _____
To have: _____
To let go: _____
To give: _____

Three years from now I'd like...

To be: _____
To have: _____
To let go: _____
To give: _____

Daydream

Four years from now I'd like...

To be: _____
To have: _____
To let go: _____
To give: _____

Five years from now I'd like...

To be: _____
To have: _____
To let go: _____
To give: _____

Decide on some very small things that you can start doing now to help you grow toward your dreams:

_____
_____
_____
_____

Max always kept a journal about all the stuff going on in their life—the good, the bad, and the ugly. They wrote about some really private things that parents shouldn't know. Well, their parents knew it was private, but they found it and read it anyway...

_____
_____
_____
_____
_____
_____
_____
_____
_____
_____
_____
_____
_____
_____
_____
_____

The Best Day

The best day I've ever experienced up to this point in my life was perhaps when...

_____
_____
_____
_____
_____
_____
_____
_____

What are all the good emotions and feelings that come back to you when you remember this experience?

_____	_____	_____
_____	_____	_____
_____	_____	_____
_____	_____	
_____		

Feeling & Emotion Vocabulary Wheel in the back of the book!

Whenever you're feeling down, you can imagine all the feelings from this day to give yourself a mental boost!

The Worst Day

The worst day I've had to endure up to this point in my life was when…

_____
_____
_____
_____
_____
_____
_____

Can negative experiences add meaning to a person's life? What wisdom have you gained from this bad day?

_____
_____
_____
_____
_____
_____
_____

Anxious

Dig up the things in your life that you feel most anxious, apprehensive, and distressed about...

_____
_____
_____
_____

Our mind spends a lot of time stuck—ruminating about the past or worrying about the future. How often does your brain "time travel" like this?

_____
_____
_____

Make it a game to catch your brain when it does this! You can say, "Brain—STOP!" Then, come back to the present moment. Say, "No time travelling!" and focus all your attention on whatever it is that you're doing. Playing this game over and over will train your brain. Worries about the past or the future will start to fade. Right now is a gift, that's why we call it the present!

Self-Assured

Illuminate all the things in your life that you feel most self-assured and confident about...

_____
_____
_____
_____
_____
_____
_____
_____

Did you always feel so confident about these things? What advice would you tell a friend to help them build up their confidence and self-esteem?

_____
_____
_____
_____

I'm not allowed to be on dating sites, but I made a profile anyway. You can't really see my face or tell it's me in the pics. Well, today someone close by matched! Now what? They started a chat and...

If I Could Have...

If I could find and procure any job that I could possibly imagine, here's what I would do and how incredible my life would be...

_____
_____
_____
_____
_____
_____
_____
_____
_____
_____
_____
_____
_____
_____
_____
_____
_____
_____

But I Can't!

But I can't have any job in the entire world. Since I'm going to need to have a job, I can choose to study and work in fields that interest me. Here are some realistic jobs I could be good at and what they might be like...

_____
_____
_____
_____
_____
_____
_____
_____

What happens to people who don't really think about a career, or who think that they'll figure something out later? Is failing to prepare really just preparing to fail?

_____
_____
_____
_____

Everyone knows that they smoke together. They brag about it all the time and are always spaced out. It was Friday afternoon. School was almost out. Then the K-9 Unit showed up. A police officer was walking the drug sniffing dog down the hall, when...

The Best

The best things about being my gender are...

_____
_____
_____
_____
_____
_____
_____

Are some of the things that you like about your gender privileges that other people don't have? What kind of hardships do other genders face that you do not?

_____
_____
_____
_____
_____

The Worst

The worst things about being my gender are...

_____
_____
_____
_____

What are some gender roles, traits, or stereotypes you think are unfair or old-fashioned?

_____
_____
_____
_____

Have you ever been mistreated based on your gender identity? How did that experience leave you feeling?

_____
_____
_____
_____

There was this guy in my grade that kept picking on a little underclassman at their locker. I kept seeing the same thing play out each afternoon before fifth period. Someone needed to stand up for this poor kid. Clearly, he was being terrorized and couldn't do anything about it. One day, I…

Family

Your family is here to help you. But they won't know you have a problem unless you tell them about it. Sometimes your family knows about a problem, but doesn't know how they can help. If you want help from others, you also have to show that you are trying to help yourself. Use this template to present a problem to your family, explain how they can help you, and how you are trying to help yourself.

My biggest problem: _____

_____

_____

_____

How others can help me: How I can help myself:

Matters

A medium problem: _____

_____

_____

How others can help me: How I can help myself:

_____   _____

_____   _____

_____   _____

_____   _____

_____   _____

A tiny problem: _____

_____

_____

How others can help me: How I can help myself:

_____   _____

_____   _____

_____   _____

_____   _____

_____   _____

I got another ticket from Mr. Wasserman for parking in the wrong place on campus. This tyranny must end! Today is the day that the oppression from these tickets will stop. I started a giant group chat and told everyone to meet up after school at Parking Lot D to devise a plan...

Shame

These are the most considerable causes of shame in my life…

_____

_____

_____

_____

What would you say to a friend about all this shame? Give yourself the same encouragement or advice that you would give to a friend or someone that you loved.

_____

_____

_____

_____

_____

_____

_____

_____

_____

_____

Pride

Here are the most significant sources of pride that I have in my life…

_____
_____
_____
_____
_____
_____
_____

A healthy amount of pride can help with achievements and success. Too much pride can hold people back. What could be the key to striking a good balance?

_____
_____
_____
_____
_____
_____
_____

There was a new kid at school. It must be terrible to move to a new place during your Senior year. They looked nervous, but were trying to do their best to hide it. At lunch, they looked dazed, standing there alone with their tray. They needed someone to…

If I Could Live...

If I could live anywhere in the world, at any time in history—here's where I would choose and all the great things about my extraordinary new life...

_____
_____
_____
_____
_____
_____
_____
_____
_____
_____
_____
_____
_____
_____
_____
_____
_____
_____
_____

But I Can't!

But I can't change where I live at this very moment. Maybe next year. Here's where I live now, what it's like, and what it means to be part of this community...

_____
_____
_____
_____
_____
_____
_____
_____
_____
_____
_____
_____
_____
_____
_____
_____
_____
_____
_____

The football guys were having a real good time at the expense of others. They were going around and asking unsuspecting people very loudly and bluntly the most personal of questions. They thought it was hilarious to make people super uncomfortable. Hilarious, that is, until they asked...

Failures & Mistakes

Look back on what you feel have been your most despairing failures or mistakes in life so far…

_____
_____
_____
_____
_____
_____

Failure can be your best teacher. Successful people will tell you that with each failure—comes the seed of an equal or greater benefit. What are some ways you can water that seed and grow from your mistakes?

_____
_____
_____
_____
_____
_____
_____
_____

Accomplishments

Recount what you believe have been your greatest accomplishments so far in life...

_____
_____
_____
_____
_____
_____

You've done all these—why not more? Outline some things you aspire to achieve in the future:

_____
_____
_____
_____

Now try this—close your eyes and visualize yourself accomplishing one of those goals. Imagine how you would feel in the moment and try to *really feel* those emotions as if they were real. Picturing yourself as victorious is a powerful way to prime your brain for success. Practice daily and believe you can achieve! When it comes to a goal, whether you think you can or whether you think you can't—you're right!

A Tale of

Taylor P.
17 years old

6 ft 1 in 175 lbs.
Kenner, Louisiana

The following is what this suspect reported in a police interview.

Taylor was with two friends at a local park located in a subdivision with a neighborhood watch. Taylor reports that he and his friends frequent the park to do homework at one of the picnic tables. The park rules displayed state that the park closes at dusk. The local police received a call by a homeowner that three kids with long hair and backpacks were in the park after dark. Officers arrived on the scene and the suspects consented to a search. Taylor was found to have a small amount of marijuana and a pipe on his person. He was handcuffed, arrested, and taken to the local police station. Taylor was charged with Possession of Marijuana, first offense, a Class B Misdemeanor crime, punishable by up to one year in jail, one year probation, and up to a $1000 fine; Possession of Drug Paraphernalia, a Class C Misdemeanor crime, punishable by up to 90 days in jail and up to a $500 fine; Curfew Violation—Violating a Park Curfew, a citation offence, punishable by a fine of $280 or community service. The case was referred to the youth peer court. As a member of the jury, what do you think the punishment for Taylor should be? You can present any punishment to the judge that you think would be suitable for the crime. Explain your reasoning in detail.

True Crime

Spring break of our senior year was finally here! Our bags were packed and ready to go. We said goodbye to our parents and hit the road. We cranked up our music playlist and were finally on our way to...

_____
_____
_____
_____
_____
_____
_____
_____
_____
_____
_____
_____
_____
_____
_____
_____
_____

The Way Things Are

Just because things are the way they are right now—doesn't mean they'll always be that way. Write about all the things you're not satisfied with in your life.

_____
_____
_____
_____
_____
_____
_____
_____
_____
_____

Accepting that "things are the way they are" can help with feeling frustrated. This is easy if you take a deep breath and remind yourself that things won't last forever. Is this true for some of the stuff you wrote?

_____
_____
_____
_____

The Way They Will Be

People are always growing and changing. That's the great thing about being human! Often, characters in stories start out one way. Then, they face challenges, learn about themselves, and grow. By the end, they're a different person. Write about your challenges, what you will learn, and the person you will grow to be.

My Letter

Write a letter to yourself in the past. You decide which age would be best. Do you have any advice you wish you could tell yourself? What are all the things you want yourself to know about the future? Give yourself the guidance you think past you needs.

_____
_____
_____
_____
_____
_____
_____
_____
_____
_____
_____
_____
_____
_____
_____
_____

to the Past

It was supposed to be a beautiful, romantic night to remember—but everything was going wrong. And I mean everything! Absolutely unbelievable. First off...

Upside Down

Write about different times when your life has been turned totally upside down…

_____
_____
_____
_____
_____
_____
_____
_____
_____

How were you able to get your life right-side up again? What advice would you give to a friend?

_____
_____
_____
_____

Right-Side Up

Keeping your life from turning upside down is best done in a preventative way. Describe some healthy things you already do to stay right-side up...

_____

_____

Describe how well you do *and* your ideal participation in these activities that keep people feeling balanced—

Exercise: _____

Sleep: _____

Nutrition: _____

Self-Care: _____ *Self-Care List in the back of the book!*

Recreation: _____

My own ideas: _____

_____

Out of My Control

These are elements of my life that I am powerless to change or control...

_____

_____

_____

_____

_____

_____

_____

How much mental energy do you spend worrying about things that are out of your control? Does it make sense to worry if you know it's out of your control?

_____

_____

_____

_____

In My Control

Here are factors in my life that I actually do have the ability to change and control...

_____
_____
_____
_____
_____
_____
_____
_____
_____

Many things in your life are a result of your actions. Sometimes, you and only you have the power to change a situation—no one is going to do it for you. You are in control of your life—so what will you do?

_____
_____
_____
_____

I thought I had a good friend, but good friends aren't supposed to turn against you. Or stab you in the back. We go way back, but then *this* happens. We were at school one day when...

_____
_____
_____
_____
_____
_____
_____
_____
_____
_____
_____
_____
_____
_____
_____
_____
_____
_____
_____
_____

If I Could Give...

If I was given ten million dollars—but only so I could give it all away, I would think very wisely and weigh my options before finally allocating funds for...

_____
_____
_____
_____
_____
_____
_____
_____
_____
_____
_____
_____
_____
_____
_____
_____
_____
_____

But I Can't!

But unfortunately, I can't just give away millions of dollars. I could generate some realistic alternatives for helping others or supporting a cause, like...

_____
_____
_____
_____
_____

What impact does helping others have on our own sense of well-being? Could generosity and kindness toward others be a key to our own happiness?

_____
_____
_____
_____
_____
_____

Hold On

Delve into all the positive things that you want to hold on to or bring into your life...

___

___

___

___

___

___

___

___

Creating an awareness of the things we want in our life is a good first step. It can be hard work to hold on to them. How can you keep the good things in your life?

___

___

___

___

___

Let Go

Unpack all the negative things in your life that you want to let go of for good...

_____
_____
_____
_____
_____
_____
_____
_____

An important part of growth is defining how we want things to be different. Now that you have a list, what can you do to start letting these things go?

_____
_____
_____
_____
_____

I'm going to miss my curfew tonight, for sure. Things got really out of hand. There was this chain of events that was totally out of my control. I ended up driving all over town on a wild-goose chase. Listen, it all started when...

_____

_____

_____

_____

_____

_____

_____

_____

_____

_____

_____

_____

_____

_____

_____

_____

_____

_____

The Best-Case

The best-case scenario that could possibly happen with a major problem I'm currently stuck with might go like this...

_____
_____
_____
_____
_____
_____
_____

Okay, if the best thing you can think of actually ended up happening—would you be good with that? Is it worth the cost of trying to fix a problem in order to get an outcome that's totally rewarding and awesome?

_____
_____
_____
_____

The Worst-Case

The worst-case scenario that I can imagine for the same problem I'm experiencing could go something like this...

_____
_____
_____
_____
_____
_____
_____
_____

Now, if the worst of the worst happened—would you be able to get through it? Would you still be okay?

_____

If the worst happened, how would it affect your life:

In one week? _____

In one month? _____

In one year? _____

Self-Care Activities

Go for a walk in nature
Turn off your phone
Write in a journal 😂
Watch the clouds or stars
Meditate
Eat a comfort food
Make a favorite quote list
Stretch or do yoga
Do your nails or a facial
Find positive affirmations
Listen to relaxing music

Do deep breathing
Eat chocolate
Take a cat nap
Create a vision board
Exercise
Take a hot bath or shower
Spend time with a friend
Give hugs
Write a gratitude list
Get a massage
Cuddle with a pet

Distraction List

Watch cute animal videos
Practice a sports move
Do a brain game
Play a video game
Do some doodling
Learn a new dance move
Smell flowers or perfume
Go down a rabbit hole

Work on a hobby
Go through your pictures
Listen to a podcast
Clean a room of the house
Read a book or magazine
Listen to loud music
Count up by 3s, 7s, or 9s
Focus on your five senses

Core Values

Teamwork	Kindness	Respect
Generosity	Courage	Honesty
Family	Humor	Security
Wisdom	Freedom	Fitness
Loyalty	Forgiveness	Creativity
Wealth	Communication	Self-Respect
Gratitude	Power	Fame
Faith	Compassion	Grace
Justice	Excitement	Intelligence
Cooperation	Patience	Friendship
Openness	Advancement	Harmony
Knowledge	Humanity	Love
Success	Diversity	Acceptance
Adventure	Excellence	Spirituality
Beauty	Strength	Leadership
Contentment	Charity	Balance
Wellness	Prosperity	Integrity
Forgiveness	Willingness	Finances
Appreciation	Happiness	Peace
_____	_____	_____
_____	_____	_____
_____	_____	_____

Add to the list with some of your own!

Feeling & Emotion

Happy
- Free: Excited, Pleased, Delighted, Optimistic, Joyful, Cheerful, Blissful
- Ecstatic: Energetic, Exhilarated, Gratified, Satisfied, Thrilled, Authentic, Worthy, Hopeful, Inspired, Exuberant, Jubilant, Gleeful, Jovial, Elated, Overjoyed

Disgust
- Repulsed: Revolted, Sickened, Revulsive, Odious, Nauseated
- Abhorrent: Detestable, Appalled
- Loathsome: Infuriated, Insulted
- Outraged: Disgruntled
- Offended, Contemptuous: Disdainful, Scorned

Peaceful
- Safe: Secure, Sound, Serene, Tranquil
- Calm: Grateful, Appreciative
- Thankful: Valued, Respected
- Accepted: Reflective, Meditative
- Thoughtful: Fulfilled, Placid
- Content: Carefree, At Ease
- Relaxed

Bad
- Bored: Indifferent, Apathetic
- Busy: Pressured, Rushed, Burdened
- Stressed: Overwhelmed, Unfocused
- Dull: Foggy, Excluded
- Rejected: Deserted, Humiliated
- Embarrassed: Mortified, Crestfallen
- Disappointed: Chagrined

Be specific.

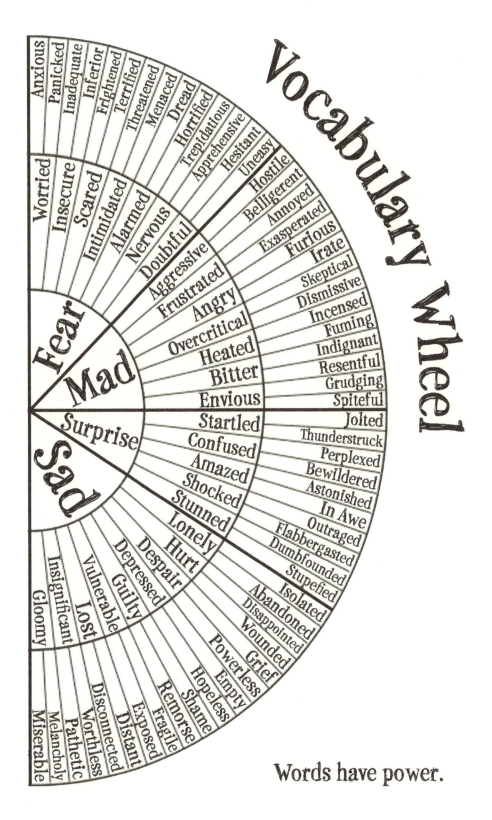

Made in the USA
Las Vegas, NV
28 February 2023

68308215R00090